This book is dedicated to the brave women who dared to stand with President Donald J. Trump, to make America great again.

It was June 16th, 2015. "ROCKIN' IN THE FREE WORLD" played.

Melania Trump led the way down the escalator with Donald behind her. They were about to announce that he was going to run for President of the United States. I was watching that moment in time, and I felt a very compelling need to find a way to help him win. I thought, "He is the right person for this time and place."

We had just completed eight years of the Obama Presidency. To many of us, the Obama era was a full out assault on everything we valued. Attacks on our country, religion, our military and police. Many Americans felt that the pride and honor to be American, had declined significantly.

We had all hoped he would help raise the black community, but his eight years ended with the black community far worse off. He even said he was there to "change America." Some called him a Trojan Horse. I just knew deep in my bones that I had to do something to protect the future of my grandchildren.

America was changing all right… rapidly, and not in a good way. There was open war on our beliefs, and everything and anybody that was pro-American. George Soros was funding hate groups to divide and conquer.

Bottom line was... it was time to stand up for, or lose America as we knew loved and honored her. Our Freedom and our very lives were at risk in my eyes.

The influence of social media was on the rise… it was the only way a grandmother taking care of her grandchildren, could get engaged while still caring for them. I needed to do something! Families needed to know that their mothers, aunts, grandmothers and sisters stood bravely to protect them.

So like all of the women in this book, I chose the platforms of Twitter and Facebook to make my opinions known. It was a new and not very kind world. Attacks were ugly and unrelenting.

I saw other women I respected, all of whom are portrayed in this collection, setting their good lives aside to also stand. I saw them attacked... I saw them belittled… I witnessed people trying to marginalize them… we all lost friends. They stood strong and did not flinch. They fought back and stayed true to their values and principles. It was a full time job trying to correct all the media lies. We shared what we learned and passed it on. We supported each other. I grew to love and respect these brave amazing women. I even now consider them friends, even though I only know many through social media.

I wanted to thank them… I wanted to honor them… but how? I decided to paint their portrait as a gift to their families... so those families would really know how much these women were appreciated and loved, and that they lived life guided unwaveringly by their convictions. They represent shining examples of strength and courage for all future generations. To those families I want to say, "Thank you for sharing her… she is a hero. She may have saved your life."

To my daughters I say, "I know you did not always understand my passion for President Trump, but I know you understand a mother's love and desire to protect her children. I know that you will stand for the principles you believe in." "Freedom is never more than one generation away from extinction."
– Ronald Reagan, 40th President of the United States.

To my Grandchildren: Christopher, Katherine, Stella and Grace… you own my heart and soul. For you I would fight and even die for. You and your mothers are what I live for. Not on my watch, will your future be marginalized. I never want to hear you say, "How did you let this happen?"

To my husband, Larry White… you have encouraged me, you have supported me emotionally, and financially throughout this process… and I deeply thank you and love you.

To my fabulous art teacher Patty Palenschat… Thank you! This would not be possible without your support and patience. Only because of your incredible talent, could we honor these women in a meaningful way.

We stand for those we love. We hate nobody. I have never met a child I did not think was beautiful, or love, but I cannot be Nana to all… I am Nana to Chris, Kate, Stella and Grace.

To the women of this book, I deeply thank, appreciate and admire each and every one of you. This collection of paintings was done with all my love, to honor each of you who dared to stand.

Make America great again is not
just some slogan.

It is what has been in his heart
since the day I met Donald Trump.

Melania Trump

Melania Trump

During the presidential debates between Hillary and our now President Trump, I learned that abortion was currently legal during the third trimester of pregnancy.

When had this happened? I had always thought it was allowed during the first trimester only, and faced with this fact, I realized this was not alright with my soul.

Now that the veil had been lifted, I started to notice many other frightful things had changed without my being aware. I could no longer allow myself to stay asleep. It was time to stand!

Amber Whitlock

Amber Whitlock

Sarah Elizabeth Huckabee Sanders is an American campaign manager and political advisor who was appointed White House Press Secretary to President Donald Trump in July 2017. She is the daughter of former Arkansas Governor Mike Huckabee.

"The President is one of the hardest workers I've ever seen and puts in long hours and long days nearly every day of the week all year long… It has been noted by reporters many times that they wish he would slow down because they sometimes have trouble keeping up with him."

"Of course he's running for re-election."

Sarah Sanders

Sarah Sanders

My father Billy Bryant, was a JFK Democrat from Alabama. He had a Masters in history, and was the youngest principal in the state of California.

My Mother Nancy Fasulo, came from a family of Italian immigrants. Her grandfather escaped socialism. When I was a child, Grandpa Fasulo warned me about propaganda, which always scared me. When I saw it being used here in the U.S. … most recently with the negative coverage of President Trump, I felt I had to take action.

I started watching the candidates from the very beginning of the 2016 campaign. When I heard Trump's plans, and how everyone treated him… how they twisted everything that he said and did… I felt an obligation to do what I could to protect our democracy, freedom of speech and liberty. I wanted to help get the word out to help make sure these freedoms were not eroded.

Nancy Hilton

Nancy Hilton

This mom-of-four, became the first woman to successfully manage a presidential campaign, and is currently the highest-ranking woman in the White House, as one of the President's most trusted advisors.

She graduated Magna Cum Laude from Trinity college in Washington, D. C., with a degree in political science. She then studied at Oxford University and was elected to the prestigious Phi Beta Kappa Honor Society. She later earned a law degree with honors from George Washington University Law School.

"I believe that Donald Trump is someone who is not fully understood for how compassionate and what a great boss he is to women."

"Hold us accountable. There's no accountability in Washington. Drain the swamp."

Kellyanne Conway

Kellyanne Conway

Lynnette Diamond Hardaway and Rochelle Silk Richardson are biological sisters from North Carolina... outspoken and loyal supporters of President Donald J Trump.

As Conservative women, they voice their opinions about media bias, political babble, and repetitive political tactics that Americans are tired of being subjected to. They use a common sense approach without the use of the political correctness so prevalent in modern day media. They speak their minds… without sound bites, and from the heart, because to do anything less would be an injustice to the supporters with whom their message resonates.

Their two most famous quotes?
"Trump's yo president, so get over it."
"We classy, and we sassy, but if you cross us, things may get a little nasty."

Diamond and Silk

Diamond and Silk

I have supported Donald Trump since he announced his candidacy for President in 2015! I knew he would win from the very beginning! He's not a politician… he's a brilliant businessman who wants to Make America Great Again! Not since Ronald Reagan's election, have we been so excited about a positive future for our country.

Cutting the tax rate for all Americans was a big first start! His dismantling of Obamacare has helped correct this single payer socialist program. He is determined to protect our borders, and has restored our military strength. Veterans are finally getting the support they deserve!

His performance with foreign countries and world leaders has once again made us number one… and finally respected again! His peace making effort with North Korea is a great start. His ability to renegotiate awful trade deals is making America more prosperous.

Finally, jobs, jobs, jobs is what he promised, and our economy is booming! We have the lowest unemployment in decades, as well as the all-time lowest unemployment for Hispanics & Blacks! We will continue to fight to keep America the Land of the Free and Home of the Brave!!

Jeannie Watson

Jeannie Watson

Nikki Haley, a Clemson University graduate, is a former member of the South Carolina House of Representatives. She went on to become the first female Governor of South Carolina, and the second Indian-American to serve as a Governor in the United States. She has just resigned her post as U.S. Ambassador to the United Nations, where she served with distinction, and was highly respected.

In 2016, Haley was named as one of the world's 100 most influential people by Time magazine.

"Do things that are uncomfortable to do. I say that because women tend to step back from things that they don't know about. And the second, most important one is, push through the fear."

Nikki Haley

Nikki Haley

I stand up for what I believe and love our President Trump! You won't believe this, but President Trump and I were born on the same day, June 14th! He's one year older!

We think so much alike, it's scary!

We both want what's best for the country and will do whatever it takes to Make it Great Again and Keep it Great!

Cathie Post

Cathie Post

My father taught my siblings and me
the importance of positive values and
a strong ethical compass.

He showed us how to be resilient, how
to deal with challenges, and how to
strive for excellence in all that we do.

He taught us that there's nothing that
we cannot accomplish if we marry
vision and passion with an enduring
work ethic.

Ivanka Trump

Ivanka Trump

When the 2016 election came around I knew I could not be silent. Our politicians needed a wake-up call, one that would shake them up enough to realize that a different course was necessary. As the GOP Presidential debates unfolded, I searched for a strong leader… a candidate who was unafraid to express his beliefs… someone not afraid of hard work, a person that could not be corrupted.

I favored one candidate, Donald J. Trump. He wasn't a professional politician, he was a successful businessman and a very strong leader who believed in God and had a loving family. He loved America as I do, was not afraid to fight for what he thought was good for his country, and he knew how to win. He believed in a strong well-equipped military, strongly supported our veterans and our country's law enforcement. He believed in strong border control to protect and keep our country safe from drugs, crime and terrorism. From that point on I did all that I could do within my circle of influence to get him elected. He has since become the best President we could have chosen to lead this country and to "Make America Great Again."

Kathy Elberg

Kathy Elberg

Certainly these are not easy times. But history does not contain very many easy times. Years from now, we will look back at this moment--when we worked to reclaim our country--and our children will ask us how we contributed to this mighty undertaking. Our story should be one of patriotic people who beat back the onslaught of radicalism with courage and commitment.

Laura Ingraham

Laura Ingraham

Candace Owens is an American conservative commentator, and activist. She is known for her pro-Trump commentary, and criticism of Black Lives Matter and the Democrat party. She is the director of Urban Engagement at Turning Point USA.

"I think that what he did in this country was the most necessary thing by killing political correctness… he stood up on a platform and he started telling the truth."

Candace Owens

Candace Owens

I knew Donald Trump would quite possibly be our next President when I saw him come down the escalator of Trump Tower in New York with his beautiful wife Melania. I liked the way he carried himself… a strong no nonsense kind of man.

I liked him more when he swept each Republican candidate aside in the debates. I liked him even more when he debated Hillary Clinton. I hoped and prayed that he would prevail.

I stayed up all election night to wait on the results, and was overjoyed to see our new President win. I am proud to see two years later, all that he has accomplished for this great country of ours. Thank you President Trump for fulfilling your promises to us.

Wendy White

Wendy White

Jeanine Ferris Pirro is an American TV personality, author,
former judge, and prosecutor. She received her J.D. degree
 at Albany Law School where she was an editor of the law
review.

She was the first female District Attorney of Westchester
County, New York, where she gained considerable visibility
in cases of domestic abuse. Pirro was also the first female
president of the New York State District Attorneys Association.
She went on to become Westchester County's first female judge.

Pirro is currently the host of Fox News Channel's "Justice with
Judge Jeanine."

"The genius of Donald Trump was recognizing that Americans
instinctively felt that the press was lying. He was the one who
put the laser focus on the press and their lack of accountability,
and America came along with him."

Judge Jeanine Pirro

Judge Jeanine Pirro

Jeanne has devoted most of her career to mastering and teaching effective communication skills as a successful writer and journalist. She also has taught, guided and inspired many who went on to enjoy their own successful careers. Like many women, she juggled being a wife, mother and business owner.

Up until 2016, Jeanne had not been involved in politics - being quite disgusted with the obvious, deep-seated corruption which filled the halls of Congress, and particularly the Obama administration. But Jeanne began to listen to Trump's speeches with growing enthusiasm, asking herself, "What can I do to help this man get elected?" She decided she would use her writing and communication skills to become a Trump Warrior. She joined over 30 pro-Trump groups, and each day she submitted short articles to 8 to 10 different groups, targeting the ones with fast-growing members. Her audience numbers swelled up to 2,000 hits per day.

This man of vision had inspired her... along with 63 million patriots across the nation. With swelling pride, Jeanne and the loyal Trump supporters saw their dream and efforts realized when Donald J Trump was sworn in as 45th President of the United States on January 20th, 2017.

"Start where you are. With what you have. Your voice matters. Do your best. Keep your eye on the prize. Stand proud."

Jeanne Arseneault Rivard

Jeanne Arseneault Rivard

In 1975, my house was bombed by Islamic terrorists because of my Christian faith.

In 2001, our country was attacked because of our Judeo-Christian beliefs.

I became an activist ever since.

Brigitte Gabriel

Brigitte Gabriel

I chose to stand with President Donald Trump because I no longer had confidence in any "politician." I had become distrustful of all their empty promises, and their alliances with special interests made me sick.

As a gay woman in the entertainment field, taking this stand has cost me relationships, both personally and professionally. I have been told because of my lifestyle and career, I "should" be liberal. I "should" support Hillary Clinton because she is a woman, and we need a woman in the White House.

Well I say I "should" be a consciously aware, nonpartisan, free thinking American. One who desires to uphold our constitution, support our public servants and military, and constantly work toward achieving the best possible United States of America. I will be forever proud to salute our flag, sing our National Anthem and be thankful to God for having the freedom to do so.

Both my father and stepfather were Marines, and my grandfather was a veteran of the Korean War. My stepfather is also a retired police officer.

Janelle Lea

Janelle Lea

Sara A. Carter is a national and international award winning investigative reporter whose stories have ranged from national security, terrorism, immigration and front line coverage of the wars in Afghanistan and Iraq.

Sara Carter exposed the Deep State.

"One of the few journalists left we can count on with the absolute truth!!"

Rush Limbaugh's quote on Sara A. Carter

Sara Carter

I voted for Trump because I knew the Obama administration, to be followed by a similar one, would be a disaster for our country. I didn't feel safe anymore.

Our then President said we were not a Christian nation, and was not standing up to other countries to defend our own, as well as depleting our military that I worked hard for, for 33 years.

Now that Trump is in office, so many of our needs have been met, including a better economy, a stronger presence in the world, and a safer country to live in.

I am feeling that our country's needs are being met, even in the face of so much opposition.

Patty Palenschat

Patty Palenschat

Maria Bartiromo is an NYU graduate, with a B.A. in journalism and economics. An American television journalist, magazine columnist, and author, who over the last two decades has become the face and voice of financial news. A pioneering broadcaster, she was the first to report live from the floor of the New York Stock Exchange.

She is currently the host of MORNINGS WITH MARIA and MARIA BARTIROMO'S WALL STREET. Bartiromo is global markets editor at Fox Business Network as well as the host of SUNDAY MORNING FUTURES WITH MARIA BARTIROMO on Fox news.

"It looks like [Donald] Trump's plan has the potential to actually move the needle on economic growth because he wants to lower taxes and lower regulations. That would be very powerful in terms of creating jobs."

Maria Bartiromo

Maria Bartiromo

I'm a patriotic woman who loves the military and police, because I'm married to a retired policeman who was also a Marine. My life has been filled with courageous men who would give their life for others! I also worked for the police department.

I believe in American values… where we all stand together and fight for our freedom.

Donald Trump was the best choice to stand and defend the proud men and women who defend us.

Jan Moody

Jan Moody

Guilfoyle graduated magna cum laude from the University of California, Davis, and received her law degree from the University of San Francisco School of Law.

Prior to entering television, she was an Assistant District Attorney in both San Francisco and Los Angeles.

"I want people to vote, I want them to pay attention. I want them to get up and go and vote and care about this country, inform themselves about the issues and I also want them to not vote for somebody just based on gender or race, based on qualification."

Kimberly Guilfoyle

Kimberly Guilfoyle

PHOTO CREDITS

Melania Trump - Official Public Portrait from her website

Amber Whitlock - by Duncan Moore

Sarah Sanders - Official Public Portrait from her website

Nancy Bryant-Hilton - by Ron Hilton

Kellyanne Conway - Official Public Portrait from her website

Diamond and Silk - Official Public Portrait from their website

Jeannie Watson - by More TV

Nikki Haley - Official Public Portrait from her website

Cathie Post - by Jim Post

Ivanka Trump - Official Public Portrait from her website

Kathy Elberg - by Stan Elberg

Laura Ingraham - Official Public Portrait from her website

Candace Owens - Official Public Portrait from her website

Wendy White - by William Ritchie

Judge Jeanine Piro - Official Public Portrait from her website

Jeanne Arsenault Rivard - self portrait

Brigitte Gabriel - Official Public Portrait from her website

Janelle Lea – by Sandra Shaw

Sara Carter - Official Public Portrait from her website

Patty Palenschat – self-portrait

Maria Bartiromo - Official Public Portrait from her website

Jan Moody - by Dave Moody

Kimberly Guilfoyle - Official Public Portrait from her website

Margaret White - by Larry White

All portraits were painted by Margaret White and Patty Palenschat

Honorable Mention

Ainsley Earhardt
Alveda King
Angela McGlowan
Ann Coulter
Arthel Neville
Catherine Herridge
Cleta Mitchell
Condoleezza Rice
Dana Loesch
Harris Faulkner
Katie Pavlich
Katrina Pierson
Kimberly Strassel

Laura Trump
Liz Wheeler
Lynne Patton
Marji Ross
Mercedes Schlapp
Michelle Easton
Michelle Malkin
Monica Crowley
Ronna McDaniel
Sharyl Attkisson
Stacey Dash
Susan Collins
Tomi Lahren

Contact the Author

www.MargaretWhite.com | midge@margaretwhite.com

www.ingramcontent.com/pod-product-compliance
Lightning Source LLC
Chambersburg PA
CBHW041133260726
48664CB00026B/535